FLOORED! SUPERCARS

ASTON MARTIN

By Jared Gall

45TH PARALLEL PRESS

Published in the United States of America by Cherry Lake Publishing Group
Ann Arbor, Michigan
www.cherrylakepublishing.com

Reading Adviser: Beth Walker Gambro, MS, Ed., Reading Consultant, Yorkville, IL

Photo Credits: © Aston Martin Lagonda, cover, title page; © LEVANTEMEDIA/Shutterstock, 3; © Aston Martin Lagonda, 4, 6–8; © Sue Thatcher/iStock, 10; © Max Earey/Shutterstock, 11; © Sue Thatcher/Shutterstock, 12–13; © Mr Paul Hanley/Dreamstime.com, 14; © Ethan Yetman/Shuttestock, 16; © Sue Thatcher/iStock.com, 18–19; © Capturing Images/Shutterstock, 20; © Art Konovalov/Shutterstock, 22; © Aston Martin Lagonda, 22; © Ethan Yetman/Shuttestock, 24; © Aston Martin Lagonda, 26, 28; Olli1800, CC BY-SA 3.0 via Wikimedia Commons, 30 (top); ZANTAFIO56 from FRANCE, CC BY-SA 2.0 via Wikimedia Commons, 30 (bottom); © Sam Moores/Shutterstock, 31 (top); © VanderWolf Images/Shutterstock, 31 (bottom)

45th Parallel Press is an imprint of Cherry Lake Publishing Group.

Library of Congress Cataloging-in-Publication Data

Names: Gall, Jared, author.
Title: Aston Martin / by Jared Gall.
Description: Ann Arbor, Michigan : 45th Parallel Press, [2025] | Series: Floored! Supercars | Audience: Grades 4-6 | Summary: "Tech and innovation are at the forefront of luxury supercars. This book explores the cool features that make Aston Martins some of the best high-performance vehicles in the world. From the history of the brand, to fast facts, and awesome photos--these books have enough to keep any car enthusiast engaged. This high-interest series is written at a low readability to aid struggling readers. Books feature educational sidebars, table of contents, glossary, index, author biography, and timeline"-- Provided by publisher.
Identifiers: LCCN 2024035959 | ISBN 9781668956601 (hardcover) | ISBN 9781668957455 (paperback) | ISBN 9781668958322 (ebook) | ISBN 9781668959190 (pdf)
Subjects: LCSH: Aston Martin automobile--History--Juvenile literature. | Aston Martin automobile--Design and construction--Juvenile literature.
Classification: LCC L215.A75 G35 2025 | DDC 629.222/2--dc23/eng/20240923
LC record available at https://lccn.loc.gov/2024035959

Printed in the United States of America

Note from Publisher: Websites change regularly, and their future contents are outside of our control. Supervise children when conducting any recommended online searches for extended learning opportunities.

ABOUT THE AUTHOR:

Jared Gall writes about cars and trucks for magazines and websites. He has driven everything from semitrucks and school buses to sports cars and supercars. He has raced off-road buggies through the desert in Mexico and Mercedes-Benzes on frozen lakes in Sweden. He has driven a lot of Mercedes-Benzes, but never an AMG One. His personal top speed is 189 miles (304.2 kilometers) per hour, set while driving a Ferrari.

Table of Contents

The Aston Martin DBS Superleggera has been made by Mercedes-Benz since 2018. Its top speed is 211 miles (340 kilometers) per hour.

CHAPTER 1

Introduction

There are many kinds of cars. They're good at different things. Minivans have lots of space. Whole families can fit. They can ride together to school. They can ride together on vacation. **Sport utility vehicles** are called SUVs. They also have lots of space. They're made to tow heavy things. They tow boats. They tow campers. They also go off-roading.

Sports cars are built to be fast. They're fun to drive. They're small. They're light. This makes them **agile**. Agile means they can turn quickly and easily. They go around corners fast.

Supercars are like sports cars. But they go even faster. Their engines have more power. They're lighter. They go faster on straight roads. They turn faster. Many are built with special metal. This makes them extra light.

Most supercars sit low. They're close to the ground. This makes them **aerodynamic**. That means they move through air easily. Imagine putting your hand out a car window. Imagine facing your palm into the wind. It would be hard to keep your hand still. But what if you lay your hand flat? It would then be

Only 22 of the Aston Martin DBR22 will be made. It is modeled after the original 1959 DBR1.

easier to hold your hand steady. Your hand is more aerodynamic when it's flat. Being aerodynamic makes supercars fast.

Have you ever seen an Aston Martin? Have you seen one on the road? If so, then you have seen a supercar! Aston Martins are special. Let's learn more!

Aston Martin's logo has wings. In 1932, the logo was redesigned. This one looks more like today's logo.

CHAPTER 2

Aston Martin History

Aston Martin started in 1913. It started in England. It had a different name. It was first called Bamford & Martin. It was founded by 2 men. Their names were Robert Bamford and Lionel Martin. Lionel Martin won a race. The race was called the Aston Clinton Hillclimb. After that, the men had an idea. They combined the race name with Martin's last name. The company became Aston Martin.

Aston Martin designed their logo in 1927. The logo has the company name. The name is on a pair of wings. Wings were inspired by airplanes. Airplanes were new back then. They were fast. They were exciting. Aston Martin cars were also fast and exciting.

David Brown Limited is a company. It built farm tractors. It bought Aston Martin. This happened in 1947. Aston Martin's next car was named the DB1. DB stood for David Brown. The next car was named the DB2. This pattern continued. Aston Martin has named cars DB ever since.

Aston Martins have always raced. The **24 Hours of Le Mans** is a famous race. It's an **endurance race**. These races last for a long time. Drivers have to stay strong. The Le Mans race lasts 24 hours. That's a whole day and night. The race starts on Saturday afternoon. It ends 24 hours later on Sunday afternoon.

A 1954 Aston Martin DB2

This Aston Martin V8 Vantage raced in 2009.

Teams have 2 or 3 drivers. They share a car. They take turns racing. When not racing, they eat. They sleep.

Winners finish the most laps. They do this in 24 hours. The Le Mans racetrack is 8.5 miles (13.7 km) long. That's 3 times more than the **NASCAR** track. NASCAR stands for the National Association for **Stock Car** Auto Racing. A stock car is a car that hasn't been changed. Nothing is added to or taken from the car. The Le Mans track is mostly made up of public roads. These roads are closed. This is done only for the race.

Aston Martin won Le Mans. This happened in 1959. The car was a DBR1. One of the drivers was Carroll Shelby. Shelby said, “Winning the 24 Hours was probably the greatest thrill I ever got out of racing.”

Aston Martin only made 5 DBR1s. Some people and companies have built **replicas**. These are copies.

Shelby always loved speed. He loved planes and cars. He trained to be a pilot. He started racing at age 29. He drove Aston Martins. He drove other supercars. He also built race cars. He built supercars. He did this for Ford.

Jessica Hawkins racing at the 2021 **W Series** championship. The W Series is an all-female F1 racing championship.

Behind the Wheel

Jessica Hawkins is a driver. She drives an Aston Martin race car. She raced go-karts at age 8. She moved to Formula 4 cars at age 19. Formula 4 cars look like **Formula 1** cars. Formula 1 cars race in Formula 1 races. They are the fastest in the world. But Formula 4 cars are slower. Hawkins is also a stunt driver. She drove in a James Bond movie. The movie was called *No Time to Die.*

She also works in F1 Academy. F1 Academy is a racing series for women. She says racing teaches lots of lessons. She said, "There can only ever be one winner. That's the reality of sport. You will likely lose more often than you win. No matter how hard you try, things won't always go the way you want them to. It's all about how you pick yourself up and go again."

Not many Aston Martin DB4s were built. Only 1,110 were made.

CHAPTER 3

Aston Martin Evolution

Aston Martin started building the DB4 in 1958. The DB4 was their most popular car. Aston Martin made them for 6 years. The company built 1,110 of them. That isn't a lot of cars. But it was a lot for Aston Martin. Ford Motor Company sells more than 1,200 pickup trucks in a day. Cars like these are cheaper. People don't buy a lot of supercars. They're expensive.

Aston Martin built the DB5 after the DB4. The DB5 made the company famous. It was used in the movie *Goldfinger. Goldfinger* is about a cool spy named James Bond. A cool spy needs a cool car. Bond's DB5 was a special model. It had tools to help him fight bad guys. Spikes came out of the wheels. They popped enemy tires. The license plates could change. This helped Bond hide. The car also had an **ejector seat**. This seat was like seats in fighter jets. It launched Bond out of the car.

Some Aston Martins don't have DB names. Their names start with the letter *V*. Aston Martin says V means something is the best. Its first V car was the Vantage. Other V cars are the Virage, Vanquish, Victor, Valour, Vulcan, Valkyrie, and Valhalla. That's a lot of Vs!

Aston Martin built the V8 Vantage. This car has a powerful engine. There's a **convertible** version. Convertibles are special cars. Their soft roofs fold down. It was called the V8 Vantage Volante. Aston Martin calls its convertibles Volantes.

The name Volante *comes from the Italian verb* volare*. It means "to fly."*

This Aston Martin DB5 appeared in the James Bond movie Goldfinger.

Normal car doors swing out. But many supercars have special doors. Their doors swing up. Aston Martin doors don't open straight out. They also don't swing up. They open up and out. They do this at an angle. These doors are called swan wing doors. They look like swans opening their wings. They have a special purpose. They clear curbs.

The DB9 was the first Aston Martin with these doors. This model was made from 2004 to 2016. Today, supercars often have special doors. They make the cars stand out.

Fast Facts

- The James Bond movies are based on books. The books were written by Ian Fleming. Fleming was a British writer.
- There are 27 James Bond movies. Aston Martins were in 14 of them.
- James Bond's Aston Martins have gadgets. Gadgets are tools. The gadgets help him get away from bad guys. One had a rocket engine. Another one could turn invisible.
- A character named Q makes James Bond's gadgets. A team at Aston Martin makes special cars. This team is also called Q.
- James Bond's code name is 007. That's pronounced "double-oh seven." Many Aston Martin race cars use the number 007.

Aston Martin built the One-77 in 2009. It built only 77 of them. That's why it was called the One-77. It was the fastest Aston Martin yet. It could go 220 miles (354 km) per hour. It cost almost $2 million.

The slowest Aston Martin was the Cygnet (SIG-net). A cygnet is a young swan. The Aston Martin Cygnet was tiny. It was built for people to drive in busy cities. It was made from a Scion iQ. The iQ is a cheap car. Aston Martin made it fancy. It made it comfortable. The Scion iQ cost $16,000. The Cygnet cost $50,000.

Aston Martin Cygnet

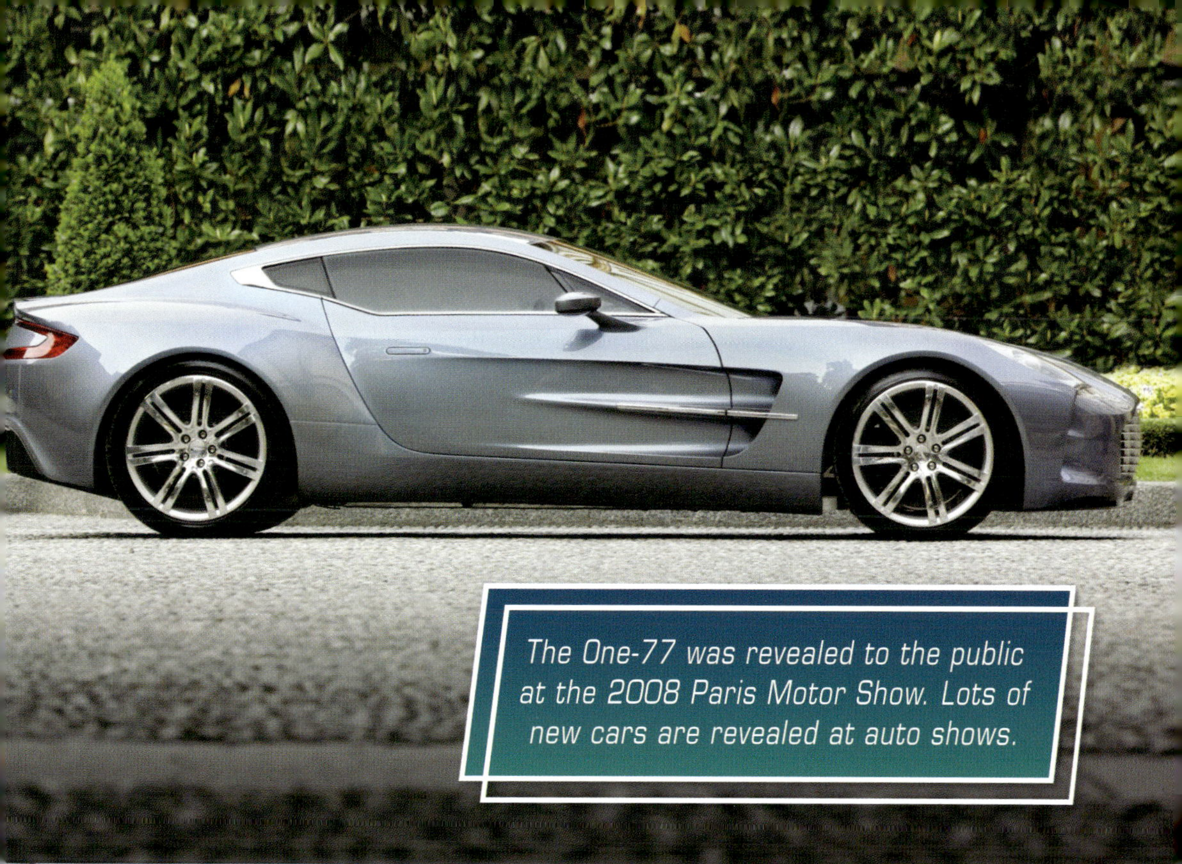

The One-77 was revealed to the public at the 2008 Paris Motor Show. Lots of new cars are revealed at auto shows.

The Aston Martin DBX isn't a supercar—but it's still really cool. It even has swan-wing doors!

CHAPTER 4

Aston Martin Today

Aston Martin built their first SUV in 2020. They gave it a DB name. It's called the DBX. More people buy the DBX than any other Aston Martin. Aston Martin sells more cars today than ever. Every Aston Martin except the DBX is a supercar. The DBX is fast for an SUV. It can go almost 200 miles (321.9 km) per hour.

The DBX's engine is made by Mercedes-Benz. Mercedes-Benz is another company. It makes supercars. Aston Martin is a very small company. It saves money by using Mercedes engines. It's expensive for car companies to build engines. But Aston Martin still makes their own engines. It does this for some special cars.

The Vantage is a 2-seat sports car. It has a Mercedes-Benz engine. It's cheap for an Aston Martin. But it's still expensive. Most cars cost less than $50,000. The Vantage costs $150,000.

A **grand tourer** is a car. It's fast and comfortable. It's designed to go at high speeds for long distances. The Aston Martin DB12 is a super tourer. There's an even more super version of the DB12. It's called the DBS. Aston Martin built the DBS engine. DBS is a name Aston Martin has used in the past. Today's DBS can go 211 miles (339.6 km) per hour.

The DBS engine has 2 ***turbochargers****! These devices give the engine more power.*

Cost of Ownership

MODEL	PRICE
2024 Toyota Camry	$27,500
2024 Honda CR-V	$31,000
2024 Ford F-150	$39,000

MODEL	PRICE
2023 Aston Martin Vantage	$147,000
2024 Aston Martin DBX	$200,000
2024 Aston Martin DB12	$248,000
2024 Aston Martin DBS	$400,000
2023 Aston Martin Valour	$1,500,000
2024 Aston Martin Valkyrie	$3,500,000

The Valhalla appears in No Time to Die*. This is a James Bond movie. The movie was made in 2021.*

The Valkyrie is Aston Martin's first **mid-engine** supercar. This means the engine is behind the driver. Other Aston Martins have their engines in front of the driver. The Valkyrie is a **hybrid**. Hybrids have gas engines and electric motors. Electric motors make hybrids faster. They also make them more **efficient**. Efficient means not wasting time or energy. Efficient cars can drive farther before needing gas.

Some buyers want an even faster Valkyrie. This car is the AMR Pro version. It costs $4 million. It can be driven on racetracks.

Aston Martin is going to race the Valkyrie. It wants to enter the Valkyrie in the Le Mans race. Maybe the company will win again. Just like it did in 1959.

In 2023, Aston Martin started making the Valhalla. The Valhalla is a mid-engine hybrid. It can be used as an everyday car. It won't be as fast as the Valkyrie. But it's still a race car.

Aston Martin is designing cars for the future. Its future cars will be mid-engines. Their cars will also be hybrid. And they'll still be cool. Will you drive an Aston Martin one day?

Timeline of a Legend

1913

Robert Bamford and Lionel Martin become partners. They start a business.

1915

Bamford and Martin name their company. The company is Aston Martin.

1947

David Brown Limited buys Aston Martin.

1948

The DB1 starts a naming pattern. This pattern continues today.

1959

Aston Martin wins the 24 Hours of Le Ma

1964

- *Goldfinger* is a James Bond movie. It's the first to feature an Aston Martin.

1979

- Aston Martin builds its first mid-engine prototype. The engine is called the Bulldog. Only 1 is made.

1987

- Ford Motor Company buys Aston Martin.

2007

- Ford sells Aston Martin.

2021

- The Valkyrie debuts. It's the fastest Aston Martin. It's the most powerful.

Find Out More

BOOKS

Abdo, Kenny. *James Bond's Aston Martin.* Minneapolis, MN: Fly!, 2023.

Savino, James. *Aston Martin Valkyrie.* Minnetonka, MN: Kaleidoscope, 2022.

WEBSITES

Search these online sources with an adult:

Aston Martin: 110 Years in the Making | Aston Martin

Aston Martin Facts for Kids | Kiddle

Glossary

24 Hours of Le Mans (twen-tee-FOR OW-uhrz uhv luh MAHNZ) a famous endurance race in France

aerodynamic (air-oh-dye-NAA-mik) able to move easily through the air

agile (AA-juhl) able to change direction quickly

convertible (kuhn-VUHR-tuh-buhl) a car with a top that can be lowered or removed

efficient (ih-FIH-shuhnt) able to be more productive with less energy

ejector seat (ih-JEK-ter SEET) a seat that can launch a driver out of the car

endurance race (in-DYUR-uhnts RAYS) a race on a closed track where cars drive at high speed for a long time

Formula 1 (FOR-myuh-luh WUHN) a racing series with the fastest race cars in the world; also called F1

grand tourer (GRAND TOOR-uhr) a car designed to drive at high speed for long distances; also called GT

hybrid (HYE-bruhd) a car with a gasoline engine and an electric motor

mid-engine (mid-EN-juhn) having the engine behind the driver

NASCAR (NAAS-kar) stands for National Association for Stock Car Auto Racing

replicas (REH-plih-kuh) copies

sport utility vehicles (SPORT yoo-TIH-luh-tee VEE-uh-kuhlz) vehicles designed to be used on rough surfaces but often used on city streets; also called SUVs

stock car (STAHK KAHR) a car used for racing that hasn't been modified from its original factory condition

supercars (SOO-puhr-kahrz) cars designed to go faster than other cars

turbochargers (TUHR-boh-chahr-juhrz) devices added to engines that give them more power

W Series (DUH-buhl-yoo SEER-eez) an all-female F1 racing championship

Index